STORIES & REFLECTIONS

FOR OUR GRANDDAUGHTERS

By *Chase Klinesteker*

Published by
Kindle Direct Publishing
Amazon.com, Inc.

Cover design and composition by Brad Hineline.
Editorial proofing by Chase Klinesteker.

Gratitude for others,
Sandra Klinesteker, Brad and Amy Hineline, Arianna Hineline, Anya Hineline

Available at Amazon.com
For more information on the author visit
chasesfishes.com or YouTube, Chase Klinesteker

ISBN 979-8-4028361-8-1

INTRODUCTION, LEAVING A LEGACY

This book is dedicated to and written for our 2 lovely granddaughters, Arianna and Anya. It is common for many mature people to wish to leave a legacy of some kind for their family and friends. Something not only to remember them by, but something that may benefit future generations. In the past I have received requests from our daughter for stories and "grandfather books" full of questions to answer about our family's past, but did not respond. At one point, I began to think about all the wonderful stories that my father used to tell me about his life growing up on the farm. Those stories of his life still linger in my mind, but with little detail. His favorite dog Shep and how he would work the cows, snowstorms where he would have to tunnel through the snow to reach the barn, horses and other animals they kept. I really regret that I did not get them recorded in some way for the enlightenment of our daughter, granddaughters, and beyond. There are many ways that life stories can be preserved, such as tape recordings, videos, or written articles. I enjoy writing, so this book is a collection of several articles written to our granddaughters about family history and practical advice on life as I see it. I try to pass on some logic and common sense in the articles, things that, at times, seem in short supply nowadays. There is even the hope that a few readers would be motivated enough to write their own stories for their loved ones.

Chase Klinesteker

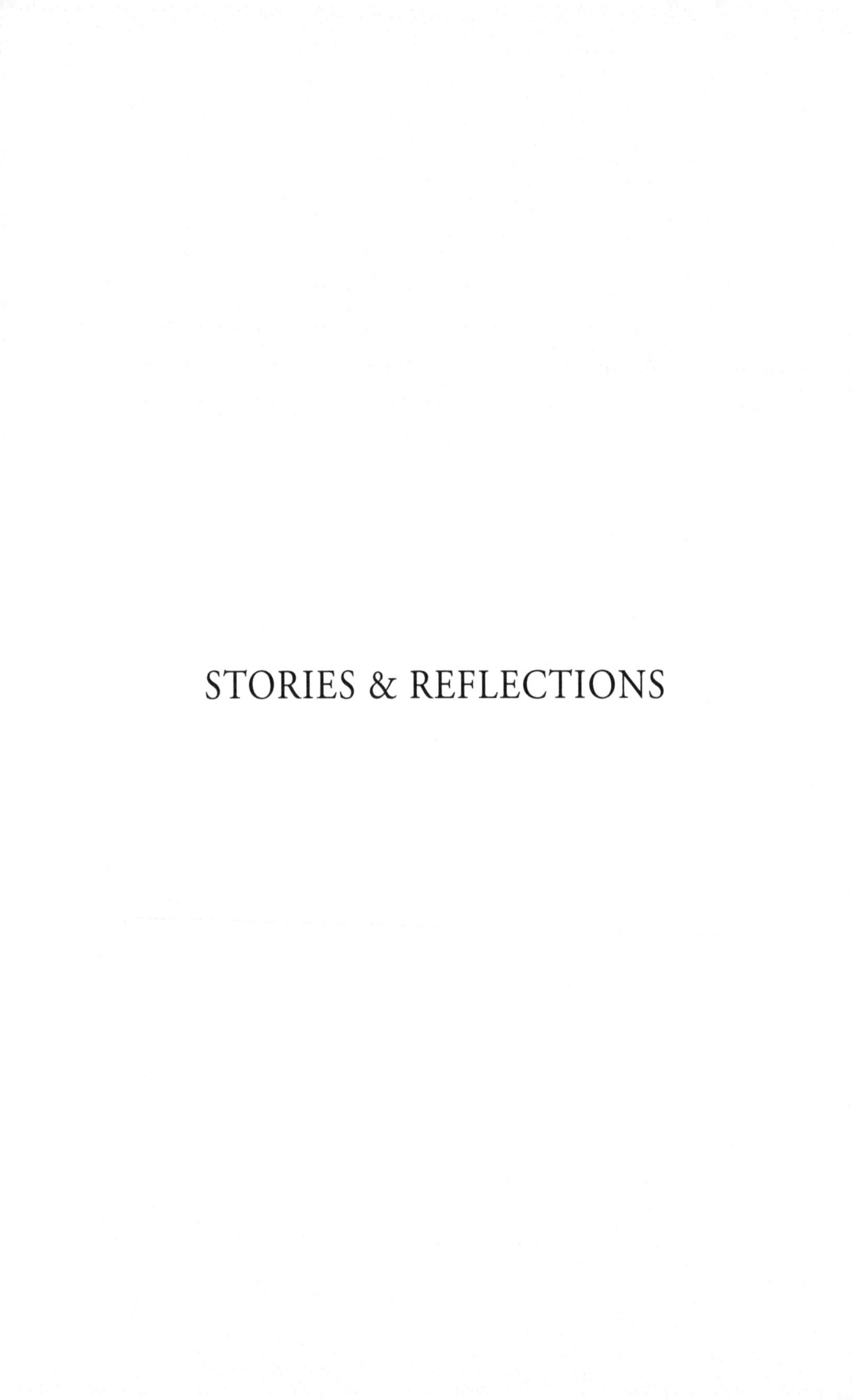

STORIES & REFLECTIONS

CHAPTERS

CHAPTERS CONTINUED

STORIES & REFLECTIONS

BE CONFIDENT IN WHO YOU ARE

One of the more common problems of many teenagers, as well as adults, is the lack of confidence in themselves. It often stems from comparing yourself to others. Confidence is acquired through life experiences. One needs to understand that each human being is a unique creation. We are fortunate in the United States to have a government system and Constitution that guarantees the freedom of choice in most areas of our lives. Instead of being told of what to do, say, and think by a powerful government (which is easier), we are given the freedom of choice. Along with that freedom comes the responsibility to make reasonable choices, as well as the possibility of failure. From failure comes learning how to improve ourselves and be more productive for society. We also can control our own thinking. Society can benefit from guidelines, laws, and thought processes that help people. However, politicians, advertisers, media, your peers, and malevolent causes seek to influence you and gain power over you. That is always present in a free society, and confidence in yourself to make reasonable choices is imperative. Without that confidence, government or other forces will be happy to fill the void. Just remember that you are a unique child of God with the potential to improve yourself and help others. You are loved by your parents, family, and friends. Believe in yourself! Don't let that potential go to waste or get swallowed up in self-pity! Believing in yourself is far more important than the perceived opinions of others.

Youngest granddaughter, Anya Hineline

STORIES & REFLECTIONS

CUT IT UP WHEN OVERWHELMED

I like to keep busy. Sometimes it seems that I have too many projects to do and I can become overwhelmed. That can be dangerous and could lead to immobility or depression, so I have gotten into the habit of making lists either on a 3x5 card or a Post-it note (I'm sure there is a digital way to do that!). Laying things out to see, then prioritizing the tasks really helps me get a better picture of things. Seeing the "bigger picture" and then breaking projects down to smaller tasks really has a calming effect. I carry this list with me at all times.

PRIORITIZING

What is most important? What must be done right away? Either put * or number tasks 1,2,3, etc. so they will be done first. Just remember to mix in a fun task or 2 once in a while as a reward. A sense of accomplishment is felt when you get to cross each task off your list when finished. There may be some items on your list that are not necessary or helpful and could be scratched off.

TIMING

Usually I am most efficient doing something the first ½ or ¾ hour that I work on it. After that I often get bored or distracted, so I sometimes put a time element on the task. Once the time is up, I move on to another task. A cell phone timer is used to remind me when I am needing to get a lot done. Most projects can be broken down into smaller tasks which are easily attainable and less overwhelming. Remember: You have control of your life. It is your choice as to what you accomplish.

STORIES & REFLECTIONS

CONTAGIOUS DISEASES

With all the talk about illegal aliens, we are missing the real danger: contagious diseases. In the past, our laws demanded that all citizens and non-citizens in the United States be checked for contagious diseases and have had proper vaccinations. This led to the United States getting control of many serious communicable diseases by using vaccinations, health programs in schools, and hospital reporting of disease incidence. We became free of many contagious diseases that plague many other countries, especially those in the Third World. If Americans travel to other countries, they are required to have certain vaccinations to protect them from getting sick and bringing in diseases when they return. Legal immigrants and legal refugees must provide proof of vaccination for measles, mumps, rubella, polio, tetanus, diphtheria, pertussis, hepatitis A and B, rotavirus, meningococcus, chicken pox, pneumonia, and seasonal flu. On top of those diseases, there has been an uptick of many other diseases also. This includes drug resistant tuberculosis, scabies, dengue fever, adenoviral conjunctivitis, botulism, cholera, cryptosporidiosis, e-coli, giardiasis, hantavirus, hemorrhagic fever, HIV/AIDS, leprosy, relapsing fever, malaria, meningoencephalitis, paratyphoid, rubella, shigellosis, syphilis, toxoplasmosis, trichinosis, tularemia, typhus, whooping cough, and Ebola. This is truly a scary list of diseases found mostly in poorer countries that cannot or do not pay as much attention to disease control as the United States. The best solution is not to allow sick people to come here to be treated or have wide open borders, as that can become a bottomless pit. Efforts to provide other countries the education and support to control those contagious diseases in their own countries results in the best outcomes. Open borders and failing to properly vet refugees coming into our country is a dangerous practice that jeopardizes the health of our entire population in the United States. Covid-19 only added to that hazard.

STORIES & REFLECTIONS

DRUGS

I like to use medicines for sickness sparingly. They all have side effects, some more than others. If your physician recommends you take a drug, become informed about it and take it if it makes sense. Never, ever take "recreational" drugs. They could lead to addictions that could cost you your life. It is very selfish to use mind-altering drugs, and there are too many other ways to enjoy life without the high risk involved. Also, alcohol should be used with much caution, if at all. Whenever you are not in full control of your senses, you may do things you could regret for a lifetime. Life is too precious to risk it in this way. Confidence and a positive self-image are needed to resist peer pressure to take drugs. It is wise to cultivate those attributes early in life.

Marijuana is known to cause hallucination and paranoia in some individuals, things not often seen with the use of alcohol. Those behaviors can result in violence or even murder. Alcohol use is frequently cited in reports of traffic deaths or violent crimes, but marijuana or other drugs, hardly ever. I suspect their involvement in criminal acts is much higher than reported due to pressure from those advocating recreational drug use. Don't succumb to peer pressure to try recreational drugs. The risks of addiction or dependence are too great. Most all of those people that die from opioid overdose began with taking a milder recreational drug first. It is stupid to want try something out to see if your genes are susceptible to its' addictive properties. It then may be too late. Smoking cigarettes, marijuana, or even vaping nicotine can be harmful to the lungs as well as addictive. Happiness and self-worth can be cultured with a positive attitude and knowledge about how the human mind and body operate. Recreational drugs can be a cop-out for the weak minded. God, your friends, and your family all love you, giving you great value and potential. Your true value is when you use that potential to be creative and help others. You only have one body and one brain, and they need to last a lifetime. It only makes sense to take care of them in the best possible way.

STORIES & REFLECTIONS

FOOD

Food is very important in life. What we eat is fuel for our bodies to build and function properly. Most should include vitamins, minerals, and all essential nutrients for optimum health. Unfortunately, much of the food available today is highly processed with fat, sugar, salt, and chemicals added. These are not only empty calories, but may also harm your health. Your body and its' health is the most important possession you have. Taste is a pleasure, but fresh fruits, vegetables, and less processed foods can taste good also, and taste can be acquired. Your mother and grandmother are very good at preparing healthy foods. Listen to what they have to say about diet and use moderation in selecting what you eat. Then special treats like chocolate, ice cream, pies, etc. become even more enjoyable. Eating excess quantities of food often (stuffing yourself) can shorten ones' life (some studies with rats show up to 40%), so use moderation there also. We often associate big meals with social events, but it is best to not overeat. Sometimes I think that Europeans have the edge on us in that. They emphasize quality, not quantity, and they take their time eating.

STORIES & REFLECTIONS

FREEDOM AND DIVERSITY

You are fortunate to live in the United States of America. Freedom is related to diversity. The more freedoms a society has, the more diverse it will be. The U.S. is considered by many to be the most free and diverse nation in the World. That is due mostly to The U.S. Constitution which guarantees individual freedoms of speech, property ownership, and trial by jury. The opposite of freedom is seen in societies governed by Socialism, Communism, or dictatorships where government often controls the behavior, speech, and lives of its population. Controlled societies lack diversity.

That diversity exists in humans is something we can all easily agree on. Diversity in size, weight, sex, race, age, religion, mental ability, opinions, goals, income, and attitude are only a few ways that we are different. We are born as individuals, and that is good. Our form of government values the individual and protects their freedoms. Without that diversity, science, research, and improvement of the human condition would stagnate, as happened in the Dark Ages. Envy and the desire to be "accepted" by others stifles diversity and causes people to stop growing and learning. Communist and dictator type governments force their people to accept uniformity for the "common good" by controlling the media with propaganda. Our Constitution states that all people are created equal and have equal opportunity to improve their lives. Our diversity comes from the freedoms that we have been guaranteed in the Bill of Rights.

FREEDOM OF SPEECH

Does the U. S. Constitution state that we have freedom of speech unless we offend someone? I believe not. Freedom of speech was put in our Constitution precisely so we could communicate our differences then work them out peacefully through the democratic process. Diversity of thought and opinion is what drives progress in our democratic, capitalistic society. When the government starts dictating what we can or cannot say or do, Socialism, Communism, or Dictatorship is not far away. It is the responsibility of each individual in a free society to avoid getting upset over diverse opinions, and to be willing to peacefully debate.

DEMOCRACY

We live in a representative democracy where we are supposed to vote our opinion on matters and leaders, then agree to abide by majority opinion. The "Me Too" and instant gratification demanded by some is driving many to not accept the results of fair elections or to condemn people without due process or trial by jury. Election fairness should be open to intense scrutiny. Nothing is more important than a true and honest vote count, and the temptations of money, control, and power in politics is high. Honesty is important for our Constitutional government and Rule of Law. The Media has much responsibility to present a balanced report of the facts in the news, but it is often biased. That leads to a slippery slope that can end in propaganda and dictatorship. It is healthy to be skeptical of all media, as they often hide the truth.

The United States Constitution begins with "We the people," and confirms its' intent to protect individuals. For nearly 220 years it has allowed this nation to grow and prosper, becoming a beacon of hope for others around the world. When "free stuff" is promised and government gets control of the economy, health care, and our lives, diversity and freedoms both suffer.

Right: Library volunteer friends of your grandmother Klinesteker

STORIES & REFLECTIONS

FRIENDSHIPS

Personal friendships are very valuable in life, but they require attention to maintain. Your mother and grandmother are both very good at maintaining contact with friends, and you can learn much from them. Studies have shown that solid friendships boost the immune system and longevity, making them very important. It pays to make an effort to keep in touch with friends. Social media can be a part of developing friendships, but face to face contact and conversation creates the most lasting ones.

STORIES & REFLECTIONS

CHANGE

Life is change. A rock changes very little over time. Living plants, animals, and humans are always changing and they each have an average "life span". Some tortoises can live up to 150 years, but I am not sure I would want a life that boring! Humans are fortunate to have an average life span of around 80 or more years, plenty of time to accomplish many goals, yet we tend to think of ourselves as timeless and don't live and appreciate life as fully as we should. Being able to adapt to a changing world is the reason humans have survived and thrived over the Millenia.

DIFFICULT

One of the most difficult things for humans to do is to adapt to change. We crave stability and security, even to the point of sometimes relinquishing control over our lives to others. It serves the individual best to learn as much as possible how to adapt to changes in our lives, rather than depend on others. Changes in life can be good, and a lot depends on our attitude towards the change. If we fear it and worry much, adapting will be more difficult. The freedoms we are given in

America allow us to have control over many changes in our lives.

ATTITUDE

With a positive attitude toward change, one will study and learn about their situation and how they might best adapt. Change is not always good, and at times can be detrimental. In America, if you perceive that harm will come from looming change, you have every right to argue strongly against it, but be civil and willing to politely debate and listen to opposing views. The most difficult change to adapt to is that which you are against, but sometimes it is necessary. The "Serenity Prayer" can be helpful in that case. Often there is a bright side, even to negative events. Most importantly, our culture, history, and individual freedoms given to us by the United States Constitution have served our citizens well for over 200 years. To change that for a one-party controlled system of government makes no sense, and history demonstrates that. If it works, don't fix it!

> "It is not the strongest of the species
> that survive, nor the most intelligent,
> but the one most responsive to change"
>
> – Charles Darwin

STORIES & REFLECTIONS

GARDENING IS INSPIRING

True beauty is hard to describe, but if anything comes close to representing it, it would be flowers with their infinite variety of colors, shapes, and sizes. Tending plants and watching things grow can be therapeutic and a lot of fun! Gardening is a very popular pastime, whether it is done to beautify your surroundings or produce fruits and vegetables. It also provides an appreciation of the wonders of life and Creation as you watch plants grow, change, and multiply. People who have grown up on a farm especially seem to enjoy gardening. Your great grandfather, Dr Russell Klinesteker, was raised on a farm in Doer, Michigan, and even after he moved to Grand Rapids, he enjoyed the hobby of growing flowers to make colorful bouquets for neighbors and friends. Your grandmother, Sandra Klinesteker grew up on a farm in southwest Iowa, and still enjoys growing flowers outdoors and houseplants indoors. Although I didn't grow up on a farm, the exposure to my fathers' interests probably led me to become interested in growing fruits and vegetables. Around 1970, after we moved into the house on Braeburn, I became interested in growing plants for food. As is usual for me, I got carried away and followed the Rodale and Ruth Stout approach to organic gardening. I bought a rototiller and collected many bags of leaves for mulch. Strawberries, blueberries, raspberries, apples, chives, and much more were tried in limited space. In 1978, after we moved to the Eastmoor house, things really took off. The new house had an adjacent ½ lot of about 65 feet X 100 feet that the previous owner had used for a large garden, so I took it over. At one time or other, I grew most common kinds of fruits and vegetables, including grapes, watermelons, muskmelons, gooseberries, pears, peaches, tomatoes, corn, squash, zucchini, peas, beans, potatoes, radishes, carrots, mint, onion, rhubarb, asparagus, beets, cucumber, sweet peppers, lettuce, and more. The experience was inspiring, educational, and healthy because I worked outdoors. When I was working in the garden, I could relax and forget about daily problems. Delicious, freshly-picked fruits and vegetables can be an added bonus to the gardening hobby which, along with flowers and plants, you can share with others.

For you, a hobby or interest like gardening could be short-lived, last a lifetime, or even become the basis for a career. All the while you will be learning, growing, and having fun! If you are so inclined, you certainly have the genes to become a great gardener!

Right: Sandra Klinesteker with Hybiscus

STORIES & REFLECTIONS

GRAND RAPIDS TABLE TENNIS HISTORY

It is no secret that my favorite sport is Table Tennis! I began playing it seriously in the mid-1980s after badly injuring my knee when playing tennis in a group at Orchard Hills Club on Crahen. I figured that table tennis would be easier on my knee. Pete Goettner, a friend from the tropical fish club, introduced me to table tennis at the downtown YMCA. I found it a challenge and lots of fun and began playing it weekly at the Grand Rapids Table Tennis Club. Dell and Connie Sweeris, national table tennis champions in the 1970s, were involved with the club. After the venue at Saint Stevens school was not available, I asked Trinity United Methodist Church if we could play there on Wednesday nights and they agreed. That was around the year 2000 and I am still running that venue. I have played in many tournaments, including 3 times in the U. S. Open held in Grand Rapids in 2010, 2012, and 2014. Dell and Connie Sweeris were instrumental in getting the U.S. Open to come to Grand Rapids and I was on the committee formed to promote it. My E-Mail list of players was used to inform local volunteers and players about the tournaments. The U.S. Open was held in DeVoss Place downtown for 5 full days with around 100 tables each time. About 700 players from around the World would come to compete. The World-class play up close was something to behold! Although I competed with players around my USATT rating (1100-1200 points), I managed to lose many of the matches. Most un-memorable was when I played singles and doubles against eight-year-old twin Asian girls and was soundly beaten! I remember watching several matches that Kanak Jha played in as a junior player. He is now one of the top U. S. players. In 2015, I did manage to win the Michigan State Championship for the "Veterans over 70" category by playing in the state tournament, although the field was not crowded with contestants.

Chase Klinesteker playing doubles at the U.S. Open.
Devos Place – Grand Rapids, Michigan.

STORIES & REFLECTIONS

HAPPINESS, SENSE OF HUMOR

One of the best mechanisms for coping with the trials of life is a good sense of humor. If you can make fun of yourself or others without offending them, you have a useful tool available to reduce stress and tension in many situations---or just simply to create a happy atmosphere. Happiness is an underlying goal of many people, yet it is difficult to define and attain. Developing a good sense of humor can be helpful in working towards that goal. Much is dependent on your attitude---about yourself, life, and others. You become what you think about all day long. If that is positive, inquisitive, and acceptive of life, you will be a happier person.

NEGATIVE THOUGHTS

Conversely, negative thoughts of hate, victimhood, worry, or failure can squash a happy attitude quickly. Don't let others control your thinking. Both positive and negative thoughts come before us daily. Sorting them out and controlling our thinking is a valuable skill to have, and a sense of humor helps facilitate that. We often take ourselves, life, or others too seriously, which can create tension, negative thoughts, or depression. Striving for perfection in our lives is unrealistic and results in frustration. If we can't laugh at ourselves, we may end up unhappy. 90% of what we worry about never happens anyway, so we need to put those thoughts in perspective. The Serenity Prayer can be very helpful in removing negative thoughts in our thinking: "God grant me the serenity to accept the things I cannot change, the courage to change the things I can, and the wisdom to know the difference". "Let God and let go" is a wise mantra.

Maybe happiness could be better described as having satisfaction with life after removing our negative thoughts and accepting reality.

DEVELOPING A SENSE OF HUMOR

A person needs to constantly work at developing and maintaining their sense of humor because the world, news, and life is constantly bombarding us with negative thoughts. I enjoy reading newspaper cartoons and rereading books of adult cartoons like: "Pickles", "Snoopy", "Far Side", "Calvin and Hobbs", "Herman", and "Peanuts". Unfortunately, cartoons and jokes are not as frequently seen in many publications as in the past, possibly because of political correctness and fear of offending anyone. If we can't laugh at ourselves or others at some of the crazy things we do as humans, life becomes too serious, boring, and negative. A good laugh can be therapeutic, healing, and a stress reducer. Maintaining a good sense of humor is similar to maintaining a positive attitude: it requires constant attention. The Internet is a good source of humor and I regularly get jokes and cartoons sent to me by E-Mail from friends. The really funny ones I often copy and paste to my "Humor" or "Joke" file in my computer. Sometimes when I am down or feeling negative, I will go to that file and read some of them for a pick-up of attitude. You may be surprised if you just start looking for the funny things we see and do in our lives. You may become what you think about!

STORIES & REFLECTIONS

HISTORY AND POLITICS

History is a reflection of human nature. Humans have a positive side and a dark side. The positive side is where knowledge, compassion, and growth advance our civilization. Hate, fear, and demonization of others is the dark side of our behavior. By being interested in and learning about history, we may be able to avoid mistakes humans have made repeatedly in the past. Then we can ignore the cries of the dark side and concentrate on the positive.

Politics is where we can most readily see the dark side of humans come forth. This is because politics involves the gaining of money, power, and control over others, which are, for some, prime reasons to lie and commit fraud. Many people believe they have the best answers for how others should behave and how government should function. That is most easily accomplished with a strong government system like communism, socialism, fascism, or dictatorship. The intention often is to help the unfortunate or poor people in society, but the reality is that freedoms are taken away from the people. Once power is gained by the politicians or bureaucracy, it is rarely given back.

By understanding history, one can see the results of different forms of government. For example, In Germany in the 1930s, the Depression had people crying for the government to do something, so the National German Socialist Workers Party was elected to power with Hitler as its leader. Promises of food, jobs, and health care were given as the Party ran the country. Hitler was an outstanding orator. Things did get better, but the freedoms of the people were taken away, including freedom of the press. Propaganda was put out to denigrate other races, especially the Jews. Gun control was implemented so the people couldn't fight the government (Jews were forbidden to own guns). The dark side of humanity was displayed in Germany with disastrous results, partly because the people feared to speak out against a powerful government, and had no recourse.

We can even see today how strong central governments have destroyed peoples' lives. Venezuela in the past was capitalist and the fourth wealthiest nation in the world, mainly due to its' huge oil reserves and production. It was thought by social planners that by government ownership of the oil companies and associated businesses, more could be done for the poor. Once the government controlled the wealth of the nation, they began managing peoples' lives and giving away "free stuff" with money taken from the "rich", who then had little motivation to produce goods and services. The result is that there are now huge food, goods, and health-care shortages in Venezuela. 1000% inflation per year causes riots against the Maduro Socialist government, which speaks of turning to Communism. Businesses around the world want nothing to do with a government that might seize their assets, causing the shortages.

I recommend that you and your sister always keep informed about what is going on in politics. Do not believe all you hear from news sources, but gather information from all sides and make up your own mind about who you will vote for. Use common sense, not emotion, to guide you. A good knowledge of history really helps. We live in a country that has the most freedoms in the world, and, with capitalism, it is an example envied by others as one of the wealthiest, most creative, and most compassionate nations on Earth. Those freedoms include the freedom of the press, religion, and speech as well as the right to assemble, petition, bear arms, equal justice, and to own private property. It focuses on promoting diversity by concentrating on the individual rather than the impersonal collective. I implore you to become familiar with our United States Constitution. It is unique and requires constant vigilance to stay effectual. To bring in a political system that takes power and freedoms away from the people is not justice. Any one-party governing system is subject to this corruption, and that could be where we are headed unless common sense and compromise are restored in our politics.

STORIES & REFLECTIONS

KEEPING UP AND TEACHING

"Keeping up with the Jones" is a crippling behavior. Trying to acquire more, bigger, and better possessions than your neighbor wastes energy and time. Acquiring skills, knowledge, and friendships is a much better use of your time and efforts. This may include the acquiring of material possessions, but for a different purpose. Learning to share your skills, knowledge, possessions, and friendships with others for their benefit is the best way to use your time. Teaching others is one way to do this, and I have gotten great satisfaction from being a fishing instructor and giving lectures at the Grand Rapids Sport Show. Your mother is a fine example of sharing as she teaches the French language. You come from a long line of teachers. My mother Bess Chase, your great grandmother, was an English teacher in Louisville, Kentucky. Her husband and your great grandfather, Dr Russell E. Klinesteker, taught all grades in a country one-room schoolhouse a year before going back to learn dentistry, and then taught at the U of M Dental School for a couple of years. Aunt Judy Vick taught as a substitute and spent many years teaching the deaf. Aunt Sally Putney Taught Speech therapy, and your grandmother Sandra taught dental hygiene at the University of Nebraska and Junior College in Grand Rapids. By teaching, one passes on the knowledge they learned in life for the benefit of others. A good teacher requires interest and enthusiasm for the subject and a desire to help others.

Chase Klinesteker teaching at the Grand Rapids Sport Show.

STORIES & REFLECTIONS

LATE "SOCIAL BLOOMER"

Try not to compare your life to those of your peers, as we all learn and grow at different rates. I was a late social bloomer in high school. I had tried out for baseball, basketball, and swimming teams, but never really excelled in any. In 9th grade, I joined the Central High swim team and swam the backstroke, but did more sinking than swimming! Currently, my definition of swimming is: "staying alive while in the water"! In tenth grade, I was on the Central High baseball team. I did some pitching and then switched to first base. I do remember in the spring of 1956, when practicing baseball up on Belnap Hill Park, we noticed some very dark clouds to the west around Standale. Later we found out that we were watching one of the deadliest tornadoes to ever strike West Michigan. I was very interested in the hobby of tropical fish and spent a lot of time learning about and working with them (I had about 12 fish tanks in my bedroom) and could have been classified as somewhat of a "loner". Getting seriously involved in a hobby was good for me, as I read, studied, and learned much. That developed study habits which helped me prepare for college, but not necessarily social skills. In my junior year of high school, I was encouraged to volunteer as assistant photographer for the school yearbook by Mr. Beatty. It required me to get to know people and take pictures of many different groups and clubs in school. Once I was exposed to all the options and possibilities in school, I joined many groups and even started dating. By the time I graduated high school, I had a long list of activities under my picture in the school yearbook and was quite socially active. I may well have over-developed my desire for social activities, as I have, at times, been accused of trying to do too much!

So, wherever you are in your social, mental, and physical development, enjoy it! Don't get all worked up that you can't match up to some of your friends in some areas. We all grow and change at different rates, and that is OK. Over the years I overcame my fear of public speaking and ended up giving seminars on fishing, fluoridation history, and tropical fish. My clumsiness in sports eventually turned into a love of table tennis at a reasonable skill level. Our form of government stresses diversity, individual rights, and freedoms that allow you to develop as you choose. It is something to cherish and take full advantage of.

STORIES & REFLECTIONS

A LIFE PARTNER

Take time and pick your life partner carefully. It helps to have many things in common, although not all will be. As you get older and gain experience, you will get better at evaluating other people. Wait to get married until you are old enough to accept its' responsibilities. Accept differences in your spouse and work with them. A good marriage requires constant attention and compromise to maintain and build. You likely will not change your spouse much, if any. We often are more critical of failings of our spouse than those of our friends, so be careful if criticizing. Treat your spouse as your closest friend, but each need some time and space for themselves. The word "Love" has the highest meaning in a marriage, as it is easy to love someone who you don't interact much with. Your grandmother and I have been married for 52 years, love and respect each other, and still work hard at maintaining our relationship. A long-time successful marriage is the most rewarding relationship a person can have.

STORIES & REFLECTIONS

PRESIDENT GERALD R. FORD

Not many individuals can say that they have the distinction of buying lunch for the President of the United States, but I could say that----kind of. In 1971, I was president of Grand Rapids (Dwight Lydel) Chapter of the Izaak Walton League of America, the first conservation organization founded in the United States (1922). At that time Gerald Ford was the Congressional Minority Leader representing Michigan's 3rd District in Kent County, and we had asked him to speak to our club concerning conservation, pollution, and administration policy. One particular bill we were supporting at that time was H. R. 10729, the Federal Environmental Pesticide Control Act of 1971. He graciously accepted and agreed to speak at our Wednesday, January 12, 1972 meeting. Our meetings were at the Downtown YMCA, just across from the Ryerson Library. We would get in line at the basement cafeteria, select our lunch, and take it on the elevator to our 2nd floor meeting room. Congressman Ford arrived in a limo where I met him, took him to the cafeteria, and bought him lunch. He was very open and cordial in his presentation and answering questions.

My father, Dr R. E. Klinesteker, was quite active in the Republican Party and knew Gerald Ford quite well. The Fords owned a cottage on the lower boardwalk at Ottawa Beach where our family had a cottage also. My father often talked about discussing politics with Congressman Ford while on the Lake Michigan beach.

The other connection to President Ford was around 1988 when we asked President Ford to be the honorary chairman of our committee to obtain a Fluoridation Commemorative Stamp for dentistry's 1995 celebration. We felt that his name and notoriety might help us influence the Citizens Stamp Advisory Committee to grant a stamp honoring 50 years of water fluoridation, which began in Grand Rapids in 1945. He agreed to the position, but the Advisory Committee decided to honor newspaper cartoons instead!

Left to Right: Ohio Congressman John Rhodes, Dr. Russell E. Klinesteker and President Gerald R. Ford.

STORIES & REFLECTIONS

RECIPE FOR SUCCESS

My wife is a very good cook. She usually uses long-established recipes that have survived the test of time, and gets consistently successful results. She follows the recipe directions "to a tea" to obtain best results. Whenever she changes or adds to the recipe, results suffer. It seems that the combination of ingredients, utensils, and procedures used in each recipe are very important as a total package. Trying to change any part can upset the end result. She does not wish to create new recipes and do a lot of research. She just wants successful results.

Spoonplugging is a time-tested recipe for consistently successful results in fishing. The ingredients are the knowledge and Guidelines that Mr. Perry has given us, the utensils are the tools that he recommends we use in our fishing, and the procedures are the presentation of lures outlined specifically in his book. Many have asked: "Why aren't my fishing results better? I believe that Spoonplugging makes total sense and I have seen the results it can produce, but I am not satisfied with my own results." After questioning these people about the equipment they use and how they present lures on the water, small details are usually found where they are not following Spoonplugging Guidelines or using the proper tools. Often they attempt to incorporate one or more other "recipes for fishing" (methods) to use along with Spoonplugging procedures, resulting in dilution and confusion. Just try to pick and choose utensils, ingredients, and baking procedures from 10 different cookie recipes and see what it tastes like! It's like trying to create your own recipe from scratch.

Spoonplugging is a TOTAL concept, a recipe for successful fishing for all species on all waters. All the knowledge, tools, and procedures must work together to produce the best results. It has been a proven success for over 60 years. Those who strictly follow the Guidelines and use the recommended tools will get the best results. Certified Spoonplugging Instructors are available for people who need help improving their knowledge, tool selection, and lure presentation. The most difficult part is getting rid of old habits and thinking. They hinder our fishing growth. Why alter or change a successful method like Spoonplugging? Just follow directions and do it!!

For success in any area of your life, using proven, established formulas to accomplish a goal is the quickest way to achievement. Learn from the past. This may require some work and effort, but then, how many "shortcuts" truly work?

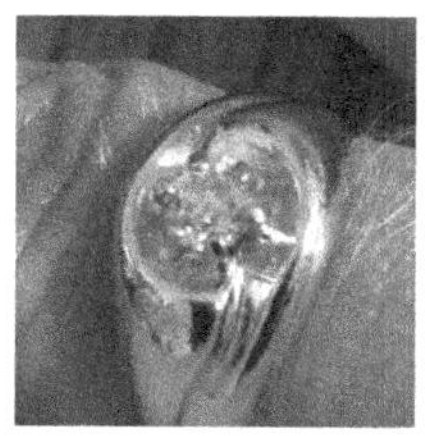

STORIES & REFLECTIONS

RING HISTORY

I strongly encourage both of my granddaughters to become more aware of their family history. The ring I wear on my right hand has an interesting story. The stone in the setting was the wedding diamond of your great-great grandmother Gertie Chase, my grandmother from Kentucky. My mother (Gertie's daughter), your great-grandmother (Betty Klinesteker), had it put in a setting for my father, Dr. Russell Edward Klinesteker, who wore it for many years. When my father passed away in 1979, my mother gave the ring to me, and I had it resized and have worn and treasured it ever since. Memorabilia items like this help keep memories alive. If we lose the memories of our family roots and history, we have lost part of ourselves. Trying to maintain a connection with your past is beneficial in many ways. It gives a person confidence in themselves and a sense of value and connectedness. Hopefully, some day, this ring and other family heirlooms will be passed on, along with the history, to be cherished by you and your sister. If you have especially fond memories of any items that I or your grandmother possess, please let us know, as we may not be aware of your interest.

STORIES & REFLECTIONS

SOCIAL MEDIA

Be wary of social media. Tweets, E-Mail, Facebook, etc. postings can be forever, as many celebrities have found out. It is too easy to say hurtful or improper things on social media. People have lost their jobs, or worse, when posting a comment that is in bad taste. You are putting it out there for the world to see. Friendships are best cultivated one-on-one in person. If you can comfortably say something face to face or in front of a hostile crowd, it is probably OK, otherwise, zip the lip! Private conversations should remain just that, as they are susceptible to being spread by gossip. My father had a favorite saying: "Never explain: Your friends don't need it, and your enemies won't believe you anyway". He also encouraged me to always tell the truth. "That way, you don't have to remember what you said". Sometimes silence is golden!

STORIES & REFLECTIONS

SOCIALISM

The feudalism seen in Europe for centuries, where leaders "protected and took care of" the peasants, was a precursor of the concept of modern-day socialism. According to AMAC, the Association of Mature American Citizens: "Socialism is a dead end. Human nature drives us to compete for success, while socialism rewards failure. Capitalism incentivizes hard work and innovation, while socialism encourages laziness and apathy. In the end, freedom outperforms socialism every time". The freedoms we have in the United States help us to attain our highest potential, while socialism stresses the state, conformity, and compliance for the "greater good", stifling incentives to produce goods and services. The freedoms we have are why the United States has led the world, and people want to migrate here. Cultures around the world vary considerably, but Globalism (One World Order) tries to put all cultures under one strong government. Mixing diverse cultures unwilling to compromise can cause serious conflict and require drastic measures to maintain control. By far, the greater good is obtained by helping people to have more freedoms and control in their own country. The closer we get to Socialism (free stuff promised from the government), the less productive and creative our society will be, and we will become poorer. When the population becomes dependent upon government handouts and the incentive to create goods and services is squashed, the end result could be the chaos as now seen in socialist Venezuela (1,000 % annual inflation with extreme shortages of goods, services, and health care). The National Socialist Party of Germany (Nazi) ran that country from 1933 to 1945. Winston Churchill noted that: "Socialism is the philosophy of failure, the creed of ignorance, and the gospel of envy."

Socialism attempts to squash diversity with government health care, income equality, laws, and bureaucracies that affect everyone, even though individuals and cultures differ greatly.

STORIES & REFLECTIONS

SODA POP

Healthy eating and drinking habits are best developed early in life, and knowledge about their effects on your body can be very helpful. Soft drinks are very popular and readily available in our society today. As a retired dentist of 43 years, I have spoken out strongly against them. This was mainly due to the high acidity of carbonated beverages and sugar that can slowly dissolve or erode away tooth enamel and dentin. However, there are other harmful effects of soft drinks that we need to be aware of.

ACIDITY

In my dental practice I would sometimes see a patient that had very sensitive teeth. When I would inquire about their use of soft drinks, they would usually answer that they drank one or more soft drinks every day, and having them eliminate pop would solve the problem. Carbonation creates an acidic solution. Our teeth are composed of a calcium carbonate crystalline structure (like Marble) which can be dissolved by acid. In dental school, we dropped an extracted tooth in a glass of Coke (PH 4.5) and it only took about 2 weeks before it completely dissolved. The effect on teeth varies with time exposure. Sipping slowly and swishing pop around for the taste does the most damage. Drinking straight through a straw does the least.

SUGAR

The sugar in some soft drinks can add to the acidity because it feeds the growth of bacterial plaque in the mouth, and their waste products are acid and cause cavities. Yet excess sugar can be even more damaging to the body. According to the AARP, a 30-year study of 118,000 men and women showed that each 12-ounce can per day of a sugar containing soft drink risks an increase of death: 7%, cancer: 5%, and cardiovascular disease: 10%. It is believed that the carbonation and sugar increase the hunger hormone ghrelin, causing people to eat more and gain weight, which likely results in the higher morbidity. The American Heart Association recommends that the maximum daily amount of sugar be 25 grams for women and 36 grams for men. 1 can of regular Coke contains 39 grams of sugar, well over the daily maximum for both.

OTHER CHEMICALS

Is diet pop the answer? Not necessarily. It still contains the carbonic acid that erodes teeth, but some feel that the artificial sweeteners used could cause cancer. On top of that, those sweeteners seem to have even a greater effect than sugar on increasing the hunger hormone and weight gain. It is ironic that the substance that is the nemesis of our environment, CO2, is ingested in great quantity in our most popular drink.

SOLUTION

The solution is to drink water, even if a slight flavor needs to be added for taste. In my opinion, even 1 can of pop daily is too much. I do not feel that government should ban the selling of pop or sweetened drinks because people need to become responsible for their actions, and that includes becoming well informed. Because we are so diverse as individuals with freedoms, the job of government should be to inform, not dictate.

STORIES & REFLECTIONS

THE "BLUE BOMB"

The first car I ever owned was a "late '48" model light blue Cadillac 2-door coupe that weighed 4200 pounds and was built like a tank. It was the first car model Cadillac made that had the "bump tail fin" where you would fill the gas tank. Although I got my drivers license at around 16, I was in my senior year in dental school when my father gave me the car. While in college, I mostly walked or rode my bike to class, so it was a big deal to have a car at college. This was the car Tom Stone and I drove out west for 6 weeks the summer between my junior and senior years of Dental School at the University of Michigan (1964). We mostly stayed in a 9x9 canvas umbrella tent at national park campgrounds. This included Bryce Canyon, Yosemite, Grand Canyon, Glacier, Grand Teton, Zion, Badlands, Rocky Mountain, Sequoia, Crater Lake, Mount Rainer, Olympic, Redwood, and Mount Rushmore. This was the trip of a lifetime I will never forget. The only night we stayed in a motel was in Las Vegas where it was 114 degrees in the shade and they had air conditioning! After graduation, I joined the U. S. Public Health Service and was assigned to the Coast Guard Base Tongue Point in Astoria, Oregon on Mobile Dental Unit #3 and drove the car out there. It was a great car, but not well suited for the mountains. Shortly after arriving, the "Blue Bomb" developed serious mechanical problems and needed parts that were not available (it was 17 years old), so I sold it and purchased a bright red Corvair with "4 on the floor", a perfect car for the mountainous terrain!

"Late '48" Model Cadillac Coup.

STORIES & REFLECTIONS

THE PERFECT SPORT

Playing sports is a great way to get needed exercise, and it can be lots of fun! Exercise is essential to keep the body healthy and in good working order. To me, it is boring to get on a treadmill or work out on machines and I would rather have fun while exercising. The sport I have picked to give me much of my exercise is table tennis. Some advantages to playing table tennis are listed below. Whatever sport you choose for exercise, make sure it is fun, aerobic, and you play it 2 or 3 times a week for long enough to get a good workout. It helps if your exercise is with other people for more fun and social interaction.

Table Tennis is the ideal sport for the following reasons:

- It is a fully International Olympic sport, and the second most popular sport in the World!
- Playing does not require huge muscles, body size, or height. Anyone can be successful
- It teaches self-discipline and sportsmanship
- At the higher levels, table tennis is a spectacular spectator sport, requiring amazing quickness, speed, and ball spin control
- Boys and girls, men and women can all play and be competitive with each other
- It can be played just for fun or as a serious sport
- It is a totally aerobic sport. Severe injury is rare.
- It requires no special clothing or equipment other than a paddle and ball
- Once tables are acquired, there is little cost to maintain the sport
- Courts (tables) can be folded up, rolled, and stored away for other use of the space
- "Ping Pong Diplomacy" of President Nixon in the '70s opened up diplomatic relations with China. It is OK to call this sport Ping Pong–that is what the Chinese call it! (Connie Sweeris was there!)
- Some studies indicate that playing table tennis later in life reduces the onset and incidence of Alzheimer's Disease and Dementia due to the continued use of hand-eye coordination skills.
- Everyone can participate in competitive table tennis. Age events in under 10 years and over 80 years exist, as well as disabled and wheelchair events. When rated, you compete against similar-rated players.

- Few other competitive aerobic sports can be played in so small a space.
- It certainly is not boring! With constant fast action, games go quickly and full matches can be completed in 15 or 20 minutes
- We should encourage churches, schools, etc. to begin table tennis sports programs and clubs. There is no other sport with as many advantages for both students and schools.
- West Michigan has several evenings and venues open for playing table tennis. For more information. (Google "Table Tennis, West Michigan")
- Players are usually very courteous; In table tennis it is customary to apologize for a lucky shot!
- It is arguably the fastest of all sports: The ball travels up to 100 mph and you are 9 feet from your apponent!

STORIES & REFLECTIONS

UNDERSTANDING OTHERS, OPENING MINDS

Openly communicating with other people, even those with whom you disagree, is a valuable skill which I hope both you and your sister will learn to cultivate. Humans are social beings. One of the greatest problems in our society today is the discord and animosity seen when discussing issues concerning society and politics. Democrat vs. Republican, conservative vs. liberal, left vs. right, etc. With help from the media, which benefits from discord, contrasts are accentuated. Stirring up controversy grabs attention, sells airtime and boosts ratings. Always be skeptical of the media---on both sides of every issue! Instead of name-calling, it would be better to openly discuss and debate policies that solve the problems of society. Of course, there is diversity of opinion on how to solve our problems, but we do not have to be immobilized by hate of the other person because they have different views. In countries where diversity of opinion is not valued (communism, fascism, dictatorships) the media is used to promote only one side (propaganda). The Constitution of the United States values individual citizens and grants them the freedom of speech to work out differences and solve problems. If we allow government or the media to control what we say or make us afraid to speak up, our freedoms will quickly disappear.

HOW TO OPEN MINDS

Instead of confronting people who have different political views than you, try to understand where they are coming from by asking them questions first. "What are your thoughts?" "Why do you believe that?" "Are there other possibilities?" "How does that work?" This gives you some understanding and time to respond. Listening is a time-honored skill used to improve social relationships, and it works. Most people will then open up and be willing to listen to your side of the issue, and you will be able to get your ideas out. Encourage them to ask you questions about your opinion. That is how a free democratic society should work. One-party governments can be detrimental to our freedoms. The United States Congress is tasked to debate issues and pass laws with input from all sides, including minority opinions. Our Constitution was designed for legislators to compromise and pass legislation beneficial to all citizens. We must insist Congress to do the job they are being paid to do! Discord results from eliminating the Senate filibuster or governing by executive order. That is not the way our democratic republic was intended to function.

STORIES & REFLECTIONS

WHY TROPICAL FISH

Many have asked me over the years why I chose to keep and breed tropical fish. Early on, I had always enjoyed keeping all kinds of animals. Turtles, frogs, tadpoles, ducklings, chicks, rabbits, and many other animals I had kept for short periods of time, but never for longer periods. My father had been raised on a farm and felt that animals, including dogs, should be kept on a farm, not in the city. However, he did allow me to keep fish, and in 1952 I bought my first aquarium, a 3 gallon stainless steel frame with green cement that I am still using today. My first fish were guppies bought from Ed, who ran the Wealthy Pet Shop, about 5 blocks away. I would spend hours there watching the fish and asking Ed questions. By the time I got to high school, I had 10 or 12 tanks in my bedroom and was breeding and trading fish. Because of a fish show I attended, I discovered there was an active Grand Rapids Aquarium Society that had a junior club, which I joined and ended up as president. Later I joined and became involved with the adult club. These were my formative years where my "addiction" to keeping and breeding fish likely solidified, and I haven't been able to find a cure since!

BENEFITS OF KEEPING TROPICAL FISH AS PETS

1. Watching fish is the most relaxing thing a person can do.
2. They are quiet and odor-free!
3. They can go a week or more without needing food or care
4. You can observe and learn about unusual animal behaviors firsthand
5. Aquariums humidify the house in winter
6. Keeping fish teaches children about the facts of life and ecological balance
7. Fish help one to understand and appreciate the wonders of science and Creation
8. You can participate in preserving and reproducing animal species that are rare, endangered, or extinct in the wild
9. Tropical fish are interesting, colorful, and decorative!

STORIES & REFLECTIONS

315 MORRIS HOME

The house I was born and lived in until graduating from high school in 1958 was 315 Morris SE in Grand Rapids, Michigan. It is in the Heritage Hill district of Grand Rapids just east of downtown. It had 16 rooms, 5 bedrooms and 5 baths, with a full basement and attic. The large, beautiful homes in this district are now kept in top condition, thanks to the heritage designation. Mom and dad sold the house around 1958 after I graduated from high school. At that time, the neighborhood was going downhill and it sold for only around $18,000., but now might go for $300,000. or more. For a while, it was poorly taken care of and multiple families lived in it, but the Heritage Hill designation for the neighborhood really helped people invest in and save these beautiful old homes. My understanding was that 315 Morris was built around 1905.

We shared a driveway with families of Dr Emil Roth on the south side and Dr Leon Bosch was on the north. The back yard was fairly small with a high cement retaining wall where it dropped down to the lower level of the home backyards on Madison Street. I remember one year when there was much rain and the wall collapsed. Also, my father was an accomplished flower gardener. He was known around the neighborhood and at the cottage for giving friends beautiful bouquets of fresh cut flowers.

My favorite place in the house was the back porch/bedroom where I slept sometimes. It was on the second floor and extended out over a patio below. There was a large beautiful Magnolia (tulip) Tree right next to the front porch which my father took a picture of and entered it into a photo contest. As I remember, that picture won and was put on the cover of "Life" Magazine. Dad had a developing darkroom in the basement and that maybe is why both Sally and I became interested in photography. His early work was in black and white, but he was one of the first in town to work with color photography, both still and home movies.

The dining room was very formal. I remember that there was an electric "call button" under the carpet in the dining room and in 2 or 3 other places around the house to call for service. In the kitchen there was a box where the name of the room would appear. The sunroom was a popular room where the round TV was!

315 Morris SE
Grand Rapids, Michigan 2008

Dining Room
Gertie and F.H. Chase, Bess

STORIES & REFLECTIONS

A LONGER LIFE

PHYSICAL ACTIVITY

Living longer is the aim of most people who have family, goals, and other things to do to enjoy life. Probably the most overlooked factor in living longer is remaining physically active. This not only includes exercise, but activity in all aspects of life, including mind, body, and spirit. Physical activity is paramount. Sitting around for a good part of the day (e.g., cell phone, computer, desk job, or watching television) is believed to cause many health problems. People with a sitting job are told to get up frequently and move around to keep blood circulation in the body. Desks with variable height are sold now for those who wish to work standing up some of the time. We know that people with injuries or recovering in the hospital are strongly encouraged in therapy to get up and move as soon as possible to get better fast. This creates good circulation and function. If there is pain or discomfort involved, a doctor or therapist should be consulted.

SOCIAL CONNECTIONS

Another "secret" to a longer life is to have good close social friendships and family. This requires close, personal contact, not just social media. The "Covid 19" virus pandemic has demonstrated to us the importance of having friends and close relationships. Lockdowns of businesses, sports, and gatherings of any size have resulted in increases in suicides, drug use, domestic abuse, and mental problems. Digital social media has not replaced in-person relationships that mean so much to us as humans. Keeping in touch with friends and family is critical, especially for mental health. Religious faith also helps many.

NUTRITIONAL FOOD

A third "secret" to a longer life is to eat proper foods. Try to look at your body (your most valuable possession) as if it were a machine or car. The fuel you use to run it needs to be high quality and usable. Old, stale gasoline of low octane should not be used in our modern cars or they won't last as long. Our bodies also need quality food that is fresher, less processed, and low in empty calories and toxins. Fresh vegetables, low fat meats, and a balance of nutrients that our body needs to function properly is best. Unfortunately, many "foods" available in grocery stores are junk and don't meet the needs of our bodies nutritionally. Our society connects eating with social events and we tend to often overeat. This places stress on our bodies' ability to extract proper nutrition. It just makes sense to learn as much as you can about proper nutrition, then do it!

STORIES & REFLECTIONS

ANCESTORS: ALBERTUS C. VAN RAALTE

Knowing some things about your ancestors gives one a sense of belonging and connection to others. One of your most famous Dutch ancestors through my father, Dr. Russell E. Klinesteker and your great grandfather, was Albertus C. Van Raalte, who founded Holland, Michigan around 1847. Conditions in the Netherlands at that time were very difficult. The country was very poor, despite being a world leader 200 years before that. In addition, Dutch leaders had a very narrow view of how religion should be practiced, even to the point of monitoring religious services and reporting to the government. They punished or jailed people that did not comply. Albertus was a pastor of the Dutch Reformed Church, which was severely discriminated against in the Netherlands. Other Dutch colonies also had religious restrictions, so he organized a group of around 100 people that wished to migrate to America so they could freely practice their religion. They arrived in New York, to Detroit, and then the Holland area on Black Lake. Being very poor, they were greatly helped by friends and churches already in America. Van Raalte was a good leader, having people skills and connections to help manage the group. Near starvation, arriving during winter cold, illness, and lack of sufficient tools and supplies were only a few of the hardships encountered.

The purchase of over 4,000 acres of land around the mouth of the Black River was mostly from large landowners in New York and local Indians under Chief Wakazoo. It was aided by several people, including Rev. Hoyt from Kalamazoo, Judge Kellogg from Allegan, and Rev. Ferry from Grand Haven. Many others helped with supplies, housing, and food for the immigrants, who pitched in and were eager to become self-sufficient.

The connection our family has to Van Raalte I believe is that a Kluinsteker daughter married a son of Albertus. My father purchased the book: "Albertus C. Van Raalte", published by Eerdmans in 1947 by Dr Albert Hyma, a U of M history professor, which commemorated the 100-year anniversary of the founding of Holland. I am passing it on to you so you will better understand about your heritage.

Albertus C. Van Raalte

STORIES & REFLECTIONS

CADILLAC ALUMINUM BOAT

When I was in grade school and high school, my mother, my 2 sisters, and I would move out to the cottage at Ottawa Beach on Black Lake (Lake Macatawa) to spend the summer. Dad would stay in Grand Rapids to work at the office and come out every Thursday evening for the weekend. For relaxation, my dad had a beautiful flower garden at the cottage and spent most of the weekends tending his garden and giving away flowers to neighbors. I would earn a little money by cutting the grass (push reel mower) and trimming the hedge (hand clippers). When I was around 13 years old, I badly wanted to get a boat and motor to go out on Black Lake. Dad was against that but said if I earned ¼ of the cost, he would get it for me. That was the motivation for my first job–picking up dead alewives from the Lake Michigan beach for the cottage association. I would get up at 4:00AM and spend a couple of hours once or twice a week using a stick with a nail on the end. For the entire summer, I earned $75! I also did some painting jobs around the cottage and some part-time work at the Ottawa Beach general store beginning at $.50 per hour. It was a big deal when I got a raise to $.75 per hour! Skip and Del Sanger were great employers, and I still keep in touch with Skip, who lives in Holland. It was a good experience and taught me a lot about money, people, and groceries.

It took me a couple of years, but I finally accumulated enough money, and dad purchased the boat and motor. It was a 14 foot Cadillac aluminum boat with a 7 ½ horsepower Evinrude motor. The boat was wide, deep, and stable for a 14 footer, and the 7 ½ horsepower motor would put it up on plane–an invitation to hot-rod!! I met a friend while out on the water who lived across the lake and had a 12-foot Wagemaker molded plywood boat and an 18 horsepower Mercury outboard, so we hot-rodded together all over Black Lake. I believe his name was Gary Eggebret. Of course, I had to get a 15 horsepower Evinrude to keep up with him, although it was a couple of years before I got that. I spent many enjoyable hours in that boat running around. I did a little fishing, but mostly running around. With the 15 horsepower, I could get up on water skis, and that was a lot of fun. It wasn't until 1972 that I got serious about fishing when a patient, Don Stephens, introduced me to Spoonplugging.

14' Aluminum Boat with 7 1/2 hp Evinrude Motor

STORIES & REFLECTIONS

CHOOSING A CAREER

Choosing a career is one of the most important decisions you will make in a lifetime, right up along with choosing a college, a life partner, and a location to settle down. It is wise to make this choice carefully considering all factors, and over a period of time.

It is important that your career choice fit your skills, abilities, and interests, as well as one that provides a comfortable income. My choice of Dentistry was in part because I loved learning about the sciences, had good hand-eye coordination skills, and enjoyed relating to people on a one-to-one basis. The fact that my father was a dentist helped, but I feel that I fit in the profession well and am still very glad I chose dentistry.

Fame and riches are not the best reasons to choose a career. Entertainment, Sports heroes, and acting all are extremely competitive, and often ruthless careers. They all have a high incidence of drug use, divorce, and suicide. Unless you have extraordinary skills and really enjoy competing, I would stay away from them. "Starving artist" is a term based in reality.

Career choices can be changed, but it is often with some difficulty.

Think about what you would like to attain in life and see if that fits. One of the highest accomplishments in life is to help others, and this can create satisfaction with your job and inner peace. Looking back, dentistry allowed me to help others by improving their oral health and smile, which is no small thing. I may not have recognized that at first, but I have received much satisfaction from doing that.

There is nothing wrong with choosing a career that does not require graduating from college, and I am not sure that results in less income for life. Some of the most successful people never went to college, but they knew what they wanted to do and were highly motivated. That is the beauty of our free and capitalistic society where creating a thing or service of value to others is usually rewarded. Be grateful, as controlled societies often select careers for their young citizens according to the needs of the state. Trade skills can allow for very comfortable incomes, and if that fits you well, it makes sense.

Hobbies create skills. With hobbies, we gain skills on how to research, learn, and create things or ideas. This helps us in our chosen careers. They are enjoyable and fun, but because of that, usually not sufficient to make a good living at. Now in retirement, I have chosen my hobbies to be my career. All the effort and time I spent enjoying my fishing and breeding tropical fish over the years can now be utilized in teaching and helping others with those interests. Continuing to grow and learn in retirement is one of the keys to a long healthy life. My website (www.chasesfishes.com) and my YouTube channel (Youtube, Chase Klinesteker) continue to help me learn through teaching others, and provide me with much satisfaction.

Getting experience doing different things in summer jobs, part-time jobs, or full-time jobs first is a wise idea. If nothing else, it serves to tell you what you do not want to do for a career. In my case, I painted homes, was a grocery store clerk, cleaned up beaches, did yardwork, worked in a photo developing lab, and was steward for 2 different fraternities over several years. After all that, working "down in the mouth" looked pretty good!

Some people Know early on what they want to do in life. Others take their time to decide, which is fine. I was seriously interested in fish and considered ichthyology (the study of fishes) my freshman year in college. Soon after I started college, I decided to go to the ichthyology department at the U of M to find out more. When they showed me rooms full of dead fish in bottles and told me much of my work would be doing scale and fin ray counts on dead fish for identification, my interest grew less! Take your time to decide a career. Make sure it fits you and is rewarding both financially and with satisfaction. Your attitude towards your career determines how much fulfillment you will derive from it.

STORIES & REFLECTIONS

COTTAGE BEDROOM SUITE

Learning about how your family might be connected to history is fun. The Philadelphia World's Fair of 1876 was the 100-year anniversary of the United States and a major event. There were 10 million visitors and 31,000 different exhibits. In 1876, Grand Rapids was a young, growing city of 26,000 people determined to expand its' furniture industry. Grand Rapids had 3 bedroom suites entered in the exhibition that drew considerable attention and resulted in putting Grand Rapids on the map as the "furniture Capital of the world". One of the suites was put in the Grand Rapids Public Museum for display. In the 1940's, my father had a friend, I think from the museum, that was trying to find a home for another one of the original suites, which was difficult because they were so enormous, tall, and heavy for a normal sized bedroom. He finally talked my dad to putting it into the cottage bedroom at Ottawa Beach because it had high ceilings, around 9 or 10 feet. The master bedroom where mom and dad slept was downstairs, with the rest of the bedrooms (3) being upstairs. I remember when I was little coming downstairs and getting into bed with mom and dad and playing with the hidden jewelry box at the foot of the bed. From what I remember and the article below, I believe the bedroom suite we had at the cottage was the one made by the Phoenix Furniture Company. It was a dark, solid mahogany and very ornate.

I believe my dad sold the cottage with the bedroom suite in it around 1960 for $8,500., a real steal! Now the cottage alone is likely worth $200,000. or more.

Article in the Grand Rapids Press in 1976 about the bedroom suites from 1876.

Dresser from the 1876 Philadelphia World's Fair,
bedroom suite at the cottage.

STORIES & REFLECTIONS

EXCHANGE STUDENT, GERMANY

The summer of 1957, I spent 2 months in Aulendorf, Germany as a summer exchange student with a German family between my junior and senior years in high school. My sister Sally had been a summer exchange student a few years before in Austria. I did not know the German language, but the 2 children in the family spoke English well. It had only been 12 years since the end of World War 2, but I did not have any memories of the war and was treated very nicely by the German people. I learned a lot and matured greatly during that trip. Ubenna, the daughter in the family, was a year younger than I, and the son, Heiko, a couple years older and attending Tubingen University. Dr. Schoene worked for the German government and the family lived in an apartment in the Gruenland Institute, an agricultural research center. I was shown much of Southern Bavaria by the daughter and son when we took bus, bike, car, and train trips around the area. We could see the Alp mountains from the Gruenland institute on a clear day. One especially memorable trip was a several-day bike trip with Heiko down to Lake Constance (Boden See) where we stayed in youth hostels. We covered many miles on bikes and I was very sore, but the scenery was beautiful. Another trip was a bus trip to Venice, Italy. It was for several days, and the tour company supplied tents for our overnight accommodations! I also visited many beautiful churches and saw some of the war damage in Munich.

At the research institute they grew fresh fruits and vegetables and I was fed a very healthy diet. My mother had emphasized that I be polite and eat everything I was fed. I must have fooled them, as one of my least favorite foods (raw tomatoes) was fed to me often.

When your mother Amy was studying French in Paris in 1989, Sandra and I visited her there and took a few days to go with her to Germany and visit Heiko and Ubenna.

Chase and Heiko at Gruenlandinstitut, 1957

STORIES & REFLECTIONS

FRANKLIN H, BESS, AND GERTIE CHASE

Your great, great grandfather was a very interesting person. He was my grandfather on my mothers' side, but I don't remember him because he died in 1941 when I was 1 year old. I do have several memorabilia from him including a World War 1 shell casing and a toolbox of woodworking tools that he used while working as an engineer on the Louisville-Nashville Railroad (L&N). Franklin smoked, and along with the smoke and coal dust from the train, he died of lung cancer at the age of 58. I also have a stamp collection he started when he was 14 years old on November 12, 1897. He was born in 1883. Franklin and Gertie, my mothers' parents, lived in Covington, Kentucky, right across the Ohio River from Cincinnati where she was born an only child. Later they moved to Louisville, Kentucky and lived in a house where they rented the upstairs apartment for extra income. My mother told us that her family was in some way related to Daniel Boone and someone in the family had his bible, possibly Aunt Floss in Florida, who was Gerties' sister. Gertie also had a sister Henrietta who lived in Iowa. Gertie was very independent and lived a long life, dying with heart problems around 1967. Krisa Putney gave her the nickname of

"Perky", and she was an avid fan of professional wrestling! She was the only grandparent I knew, as my fathers' parents both died before I was born.

Franklin H, Bess, and Gertie Chase

STORIES & REFLECTIONS

GLOBAL WARMING

According to some, we will all be dead in 10 years from global warming. In 1972 when I was president of the local chapter of the Izaak Walton League (one of Americas' first environmental organizations), the scientist "experts" of the day were telling us that global cooling would kill us all by 1990 (along with the population time bomb). It was felt at the time that excess carbon dioxide in the atmosphere would block out sunlight and cause the earth to cool so much that crops could not be grown.

GEOLOGIC HISTORY

Of course, that didn't happen, and now the "scientific experts" are telling us that global warming will destroy the earth in even less time than they predicted before. I have my doubts about that. Climate change has happened throughout the Earths' geologic history. Michigan was once entirely covered with ice and before that, a warm tropical sea. Predictions involve guesses of what will happen in the future, and it is nearly impossible to predict what will happen in such a complex ecosystem involving life, biology, and astronomical factors.

Just one factor like sunspot activity can upset the long term warming or cooling of our planet. Scientific knowledge will expand when we reach "the future" and that may negate predictions of scientists (e.g. "global cooling").

CONFIDENCE IN HUMANITY

Environmental science is an ongoing study. We are constantly learning and adapting to that knowledge. As civilization advances, it changes, usually for the better. For example, in Europe and the United States, family sizes are small and there is little or no population growth, but in Third World countries most families are large. The advance of civilized values and knowledge creates less need or desire for large families. By bringing modern technology to third world countries, we will make their lives better and avoid the "Population Time Bomb". Scientific advances in plant cultivation and farming clearly have allowed for better and more food production, as well as soil preservation. Humans have survived and thrived over the millennia because of their ability to adapt and innovate. Almost all the main disasters in human history have been the result of powerful dictatorial governments who slaughtered their own citizens or those in countries they conquered. There was no U S Constitution or freedoms given to those citizens.

FREEDOM RESULTS IN PROGRESS

I am not against protecting the environment, but we need to use common sense before we destroy our country and way of life. Much of the Third World needs to catch up to what we are already doing to protect the environment. One World Order scares me. If the United States hadn't entered the Second World War when we did (global cooperation), we likely would now have global government and all be speaking German or Japanese, with freedoms lost under a dictatorship. Let us use common sense in what we do to protect our environment. Soil conservation, reducing water pollution, and using some alternative energy sources, all can be done without destroying our economic lives. What we need to do is encourage modernization in culture and technology of third-world countries so they can benefit as we have.

BE SKEPTICAL OF "SCIENTIFIC FACTS"

Fears of Polar Bear decimation may be unfounded. Forecasting the future can be very difficult, and statistics can be made to support just about anything. One established fact is that Polar Bear numbers have doubled in Canada over the last 30 years, reaching a new high of 29,500 in 2018 (https://www.thegwpf.org/new-report-polar-bears-continue-to-thrive/). In fact, there are requests from native Canadians for the government to reduce the bear population due to increased bear attacks on humans.

STORIES & REFLECTIONS

GO WEST, YOUNG MAN

The summer of 1963 when I was in dental school, I decided to take a trip out west with a friend from high school, Tom Stone. We both painted houses for a few weeks that summer before we left in order to earn some money. Tom's father owned some apartment houses that we worked on and painted. My father let us take the "Blue Bomb", a late 1948 2-door, 4200 pound Cadillac coupe that got 8 miles per gallon of gas. It was a low budget trip, so we purchased a 9x9 green canvas umbrella tent and stayed in campgrounds of National Parks most nights. It really helped that gas prices were only 30 cents per gallon! We covered over 6,000 miles in 6 weeks that summer visiting many national parks, including Bryce Canyon, Yosemite, Grand Canyon, Glacier, Grand Teton, Zion, Badlands, Rocky Mountain, Sequoia, Crater Lake, Mount Rainer, Olympic, Redwood, Hoover Dam, Estes Park, Yellowstone, Dinosaur National Monument, and Mount Rushmore. This was the trip of a lifetime I will never forget. We started with the southern route (Route 66) to Los Angeles, California, then up the West Coast 101 to Seattle, and back across the northern states. The only night we stayed in a motel was in Las Vegas where it was 114 degrees in the shade and they had air conditioning!

Top: Tom Stone, ready to chop down a California Redwood.
Bottom: 9x9 umbrella tent in campground.

STORIES & REFLECTIONS

IN THE SPOTLIGHT

Most people do not crave to be in the center of attention. A few have that quality where they enjoy being in the spotlight and are outgoing, but the great majority prefer to stay on the sidelines and live their life quietly. Yet striving to develop skills relating to being in front of other people can benefit us greatly. Speaking and leadership skills greatly enhance our ability to accomplish goals and get things done. As a young dentist, I was shy and lacked self-confidence. I just wanted to quietly do my work. At a local dental meeting I was encouraged to attend a Dental Toastmasters meeting that was focused on learning speaking skills. It was scary at first, as we were required to get up in front of the group and talk about a subject for a minute or two and then be critiqued by the others. We started with subjects we were familiar with, then later were given random subjects to help us think on our feet. It was difficult, but later on I became more comfortable being in front of people and speaking. That first step to attend the Toastmasters meeting was one of the more significant decisions in my life. It helped me to expand my horizons greatly, even helping to relate better with my patients and have more confidence. As knowledge increased, I was better equipped to share it with others and take on leadership roles. The more knowledge gained on a subject, the more relaxed and confident I was in speaking to others about it. This was also true with hobby interests such as fishing and breeding tropical fish. I became motivated to teach and inform others on what I had learned. Writing articles about these subjects helped to share with others, and eventually educational websites (chasesfishes.com) and You-Tube channel were produced.

What you wish to do with your life relies heavily on the skills that you develop. Being comfortable in front of others and a willingness to speak out are valuable skills for anyone to have.

Speaking at the ADA 70th Anniversary Symposium for Water Fluridation

STORIES & REFLECTIONS

LIVE UNDER YOUR MEANS

Financial worries are one of the biggest causes of stress in our lives today. One of the most important keys to happiness is to live under your means by spending less than you earn and saving for the future. When we compare ourselves to others, we tend to want bigger and more expensive goods and services. Yet there are many choices out there where we can reduce or eliminate costs, especially on things that are not essential. The overuse of credit cards is often the culprit. It is more difficult to write a check or pay in cash, but doing so allows you to keep better track of your finances and debt. It is best to pay off our credit card bill in full every month. If it can't be paid off, one must reduce spending or debt can easily spiral out of control. I grew up in the 1940's and 1950's when credit cards were unknown, or used very little, and most all purchases were in cash or by check. If we didn't have the cash, we wouldn't buy it! Life is much more complex nowadays. There are infinitely more choices of things to spend money on and many different ways to pay or borrow. We have redefined what we consider "essential".

My parents lived through World War 1, the Great Depression, and World War 2, and were emphatic that I understand the seriousness of being heavily in debt. Americans living nowadays have not experienced serious depression, hunger, or poverty that was prevalent then, so they cannot envision those consequences. Yet we may be even more susceptible to financial ruin now than before, due to the excesses in our society today. The best way to prepare for a financial downturn is to start saving early in the form of personal investments, IRA, pensions, or even some real estate. Start small and diversify to spread the risk. If you aren't interested in financial matters, get trustworthy advisors, but the more you learn and understand, the better your results will be. Always remember, YOU are in control of the results, and your advisors must thoroughly explain why certain investments are recommended. Don't count on your job, a pension, social security, or the government to take care of you after you retire. With businesses closing, inflation, and new legislation, history has often proven that a false hope.

I have made some poor financial decisions in the past where I didn't thoroughly explore my options or trusted individuals I shouldn't have, but became better informed because of that. Those advocating communal ownership (communism) will try to make you feel guilty if you work hard to save and become "rich". Just remember: your primary responsibility is to yourself and your family. No one else can fill that gap. It is a struggle to save for the future, but a financially secure retirement allows you and your family to be in control and enjoy life, as well as to share it with others less fortunate.

STORIES & REFLECTIONS

HEALTH = MOVEMENT AND MOTIVATION

Most people seem to know individuals that defy the rules of keeping healthy. There are some people that are overweight, smoke, drink, don't exercise, or eat unhealthy foods, yet seem to be quite healthy. We often comment that this will catch up to them at some point, and often it does. Yet how do we explain that some people who are older still have some of these bad habits and are very healthy? President Trump may be one of them. He doesn't smoke or drink alcohol, but he may not do regular exercise, is somewhat overweight, gets little sleep, and often eats junk food. Yet at 72 years old, he ran circles around his political opponents. He manages to get more done in one day than 3 people, and his staff complains that they can't keep up with him. Rather than criticize another persons' behavior, it would be wise to try and understand how this can happen. What are the factors that allow people, despite some "bad" habits, to stay healthy and be active? I suspect that movement and motivation are two key factors.

MOVEMENT

To accomplish anything, movement is usually necessary. The human body is designed to move, with joints and blood circulation needed to keep it moving. Generally, people with sedentary jobs are known to have more health problems, and health experts emphasize that exercise is essential. But how much and what kind of exercise is best? The answer may be more general, and that movement is the key to staying healthy. Movement can include walking around or just being on your feet. The more things planned for the day, the more movement you get. Keep moving to keep going. I like the moto: "I would rather wear out than rust out."

MOTIVATION

Motivation is a bit harder to define. It could be thought of as a strong desire to accomplish objectives, or get things done. It is usually thought of as a positive attitude where one is having fun, attaining goals, and helping others. It can be a driving force that gets people to take action, rather than just a desire to do something. Positive self-motivation usually comes from within and is a developed skill or habit which helps a person get things done. Fear of consequences is also a motivator. It often is needed when self-motivation has not resulted in action. Negative motivation, where one uses hate, fear, or discrediting other people is mostly destructive. It is best to try and develop your own positive self-motivating habits.

HOW IS MOTIVATION DEVELOPED?

It starts with the understanding that only you can change your own behavior. Your desire to improve yourself and help others is the driving force of motivation. It usually comes from within yourself, so you can't depend on others to motivate you. Hate, fear, and victimhood are sometimes used by others to try and motivate you to do what they want, but positive self-motivation is best to help you attain your own goals. Writing down your goals, reading self-help books, and choosing friends who are positive are some ways that can help. Believe in yourself and your God-given ability to accomplish goals and help others. Your attitude toward life is the key ingredient. Attitude is something we can control. Keep it realistic yet positive. A positive attitude towards yourself and life in general goes a long way in helping you get motivated. It is something you choose to have!

ATTITUDE – by Charles Swindoll

"The longer I live, the more I realize the impact of attitude on life. Attitude, to me, is more important than facts. It is more important than the past, than education, than money, than circumstances, than failures, than success, than what other people think or say or do. It is more important than appearance, giftedness, or skill. It will make or break a company…a church…a home. The remarkable thing is we have a choice every day regarding the attitude we will embrace for that day. We cannot change our past…we cannot change the fact that people will act in a certain way. We cannot change the inevitable. The only thing we can do is play on the one string we have, and that is our attitude. I am convinced that life is 10% of what happens to me and 90% how I react to it. And so it is with you…we are in charge of our ATTITUDES."

STORIES & REFLECTIONS

MY FIRST BOWL

One object I remember making in grade school was a ceramic bowl or ash tray. My mother still smoked at that time, although my father had quit several years before. It was common for kids to make ash trays for their parents in art class. I attended Lafayette Grade School on the corner of Cherry and Lafayette streets in Grand Rapids. The name was later changed to Authur H Vandenberg Grade School. Vandenberg was a famous United States senator who had much influence on the formation of the Marshall Plan which helped rebuild Europe after World War 2. He lived in the home across the street from us and my sister Judy got to know him. The school was around 5 or 6 blocks from our home at 315 Morris, which we walked every day. In art class they had a large kiln to fire clay ceramics and we were tasked with creating something. Projects were formed by hand in clay and fired, then painted, glazed, and refired to set the glaze. I enjoyed doing that and liked to work with my hands. Being creative and working with your hands can be therapeutic and very satisfying, and I found that helpful later in life for my profession and hobbies.

STORIES & REFLECTIONS

RETIREMENT IS FOR HELPING OTHERS

As a young adult, you probably have little thought about retirement. It seems a long way off, but at some point in your life, you will be facing retirement. Often when a person retires, the first thing they say they want to do is to do things to have fun. Traveling and enjoying hobbies are two of the most often mentioned. That is fine and deserved, but at some point there is a realization that there is more to life than that. For all stages of life, true satisfaction comes from being helpful to others, giving one a sense of self-worth. Most of us worked at jobs that contributed to society in some way, and when we retire, there is a void in that area. There are many ways to help others, including creating goods, services, or just plain helping others with your time, money, or talents.

Plan for an active retirement with plenty of activities and interests. It is far better to "wear out" than to "rust out", and you will likely live longer also! The last thing you want is to become sedentary or a couch potato. The human body is made to move, function, and get things done. "Use it or lose it" is a mantra often applied to our abilities, both mental and physical.

The first thing one thinks about when helping others is to give to the poor and those in unfortunate circumstances. That is exemplary. More helpful to them would be to teach them skills on how to increase their income or better their circumstances. I really admire teachers. Knowledge and skills help one to better themselves and become more independent. This will give an immeasurable boost in self-worth and help them contribute to society.

Retirement is for helping others and leaving "footprints" that will last long after you are gone. My hope is that some of the things I am doing will leave lasting thoughts that serve that purpose.

STORIES & REFLECTIONS

SOCIETY IS CHANGING

Society is culture, and that is something that changes over time. Cultures that have survived over long periods of time (e.g. Greece, Rome, China, Egypt, etc.) seem to have rules, discipline, and beliefs that survive to protect the culture from changing too fast. Religion is one factor that plays a big role. It usually is the moral basis for a culture. Anthropology studies indicate that a belief system is basic. When things change too fast for people to reasonably adjust, anarchy can result.

The emphasis on diversity in America has made changes occur faster in our society. American culture has developed over many years by incorporating the many cultures from a diverse variety of immigrants, yet there was a distinct American culture that was recognized and sought after around the world. Cultures vary considerably in their customs, behaviors, and beliefs. The variety is so wide-ranging that just communicating and getting along together is difficult if not impossible for some. Stability is gained by countries having borders and a culture where most individuals speak the same language and think somewhat alike. We would like to think that all humans should just be able to just get along under one government, but that has proven to be impossible unless a powerful government dictates what that culture will be and how people must behave. That would not play well with our diverse American culture, which values the individual freedoms of speech, religion, property ownership, and equal protection under the law.

The current turmoil in our country is related to a group of individuals who would like to vastly and quickly change our culture from the Judeo-Christian values of hard work, individualism, and freedoms to a restrictive totalitarian state (Marxism). The religious foundation our country was formed under has been eroding. Observing the rioters and looters, one could assume they have little respect for private property or the lives of people who think differently than they do. They complain about the greed associated with capitalism, and then show their own greed by robbing and looting the possessions of others, whether illegally or by government confiscation. Violent intimidation and fear are used to keep citizens quiet. If we value our culture in America, we will stand up and speak out against these Marxist anarchists. The United States of America has held a World leadership role in science, freedoms, philanthropy, and economy for many years. To throw that away to placate an angry mob or because of dislike for a certain politician does not make sense.

STORIES & REFLECTIONS

"STICKS AND STONES"

One of the most remembered sayings of my childhood was: "Sticks and stones can break my bones but words will never hurt me". I can't remember where I picked that up, but it was useful to me, especially around bullies. My parents had helped me develop enough self-confidence so that whatever someone else said about me, I would not be offended or get upset. It was their problem, not mine. I was little bigger than a 100-pound weakling, but not by much, and got my share of verbal bullying from some classmates. I simply refused to let others control me or my emotions. Physical harm was another thing, and I got good and fast on my feet!

ARE YOU OFFENDED?

Today, too many people get upset or offended by what other people say. They demand that others be punished or be fired from their jobs for a few words said in anger or written on social media. Since when is one persons' opinion of you that important? Get used to it. Bullies are a fact of life, and the sooner you learn to brush them off, the better. They usually do it because they have a poor self-image, and it gives them attention. Politics is one occupation that can attract bullies because it involves controlling others. No matter what party, always be skeptical of what politicians say, and never allow them to gain much power over you. When they promise "free stuff" using other people's money, watch out.

FREEDOMS

Freedom of speech is the most important freedom our Constitution and Bill of Rights guarantees American citizens. All totalitarian governments restrict free speech, especially negative things said about the government or political leaders. Censorship in free societies can slowly increase and end up with government in complete control. Nowadays, monopolistic social and news media can collude with politicians to remove any bad things said about our leaders, which squashes free speech and gives government more power and control.

THE SOLUTION

The solution is to speak up, be honest, and use common sense. Be willing to debate issues politely. Violence and property damage is illegal, and not part of free speech. Those people not willing to discuss issues calmly are too emotional, and likely have poor arguments anyway. Remember, freedom of speech throughout human history has been rare. Savor and protect the United States Constitution. It is not guaranteed unless we hold it close.

STORIES & REFLECTIONS

STRIVE TO CREATE

Teens often struggle with boredom, depression, or anxiety, which can lead to more serious issues, even suicide. This could be due to them not having enough life experiences to give them some knowledge and self-confidence. As they move into their 20's and older, the suicide incidence seems to decrease. How does one gain self-confidence? I believe that one key solution might be to strive to create. I am using a very broad definition of the word "create" to include learning, building things, and helping others. It could even include exercise, as you are creating a healthier body. Moving forward and gaining life experiences is something you will be doing all your life, and that is essential to maintaining a healthy mental state.

BEING CREATIVE

To be creative, one often needs to take some risk. For example, communicating with a friend on Facebook requires little risk, but a call, handwritten letter, or meeting in person involves more risk----and is much more meaningful, often resulting in experiences or memories that are lasting. When you create friends, experiences, or help others, it opens you up to a wider world that is more interesting and exciting. It takes one away from the self-pity and negative thoughts that can destroy lives. Negativity often results when we compare ourselves to others or look for their approval. Motivation to create must come from within you, but it helps you to live a fuller, more satisfying life.

CHANGE

Life could be equated with change. Just as every cell in our bodies is growing, reproducing, and sloughing, our lives move forward with changes. Change can be threatening, and humans naturally prefer stability, but sometimes we need to face reality and adjust. I find great strength in the Serenity Prayer, which encourages us to solve problems, but to put in God's hands those things we can't control. Common sense toward our problems is also gained through creative life experiences.

DIVERSITY

Be thankful that you live in a country that encourages diversity and has freedoms that allow your creative talents to blossom. People who live in more controlled and homogenous societies do not have the opportunity that you do to create and experience many of the joys in life.

STORIES & REFLECTIONS

THE 1918 FLU PANDEMIC

The most severe flu pandemic in recorded history started in March of 1918. It claimed at least 50 million lives worldwide. This number is greater than the total number of military and civilian deaths suffered during all of World War 1. Living in close quarters and more global travel seemed to increase its' spread. It was a virulent and deadly virus that mutated from contact with a bird, and people had little resistance to it. Your great grandfather (and my father) Russell Klinesteker caught it and almost died when he was in college in 1918. He said that a lady who lived close by came over to his apartment every day to feed, care, and clean up for him, and that he was so sick that he likely would have died had she not helped him. That flu was contagious and there were few people willing to do that. She was a real angel in disguise, and if she had not helped him, you and I would likely not have been born!

It was found with the 1918 pandemic that in those cities which limited large gatherings of people, there were fewer infections. I strongly believe in using vaccines and all the advances in disease research. I was given the polio vaccine which protected me from that devastating disease. Before the vaccine came out, I remember my parents severely restricted my outdoor activities to avoid catching polio. I urge you to study and learn about diseases and vaccines. The more you know, the better choices you will make regarding disease prevention and treatment. Getting involved in emotional speculation about vaccines does not make sense when proven research and modern treatments are available. Science in a free, democratic, and open society is very believable. Under a one-party governing system where politics control the flow of information, however, it can be suspect.

STORIES & REFLECTIONS

TYRANNY OF THE MONOPOLY

Politics is important. I recommend you both learn about our freedoms and how government works. Just make sure you listen to both sides and make your own conclusions, as media are often biased. Monopolies form naturally in a free society but are not in the best interests of the people. Once control of a market is obtained, fraud and deceit are often used to control products and prices, and competition is eliminated. For capitalism to function properly, monopolies must be curtailed. There are many anti-trust laws in the United States that were passed to break up monopolies and encourage competition (e.g. Ma Bell etc.), but there is little enforcement of those laws today. Perhaps it would be wise to re-examine those laws with the intent to increase competition. Also, governments can become monopolies that control peoples' lives when basic freedoms are not granted to their citizens.

According to past Attorney General William Barr, there are 3 bulwarks that prevent countries from turning into an oppressive dictatorship, where government can be described as having a monopoly controlling peoples' lives.

1) RELIGION.

All major world religions have moral guidelines for treating our fellow humans in a compassionate way. These guidelines are critical and found pretty much in all societies. When governments restrict or remove the freedom of religion, oppression reigns. Hitler, Mao Tso Tung, Stalin, and many others in history removed religion from their countries, and were worshiped as gods themselves. Speech suppression prevailed, and killing people meant nothing to them if it helped them maintain their power.

2) DECENTRALIZATION OF GOVERNMENT POWER

The United States Constitution only gives limited powers to the Federal Government and the remaining functions are granted to the individual states. The three equal branches of government (executive, legislative, and judicial), make it more difficult to concentrate power in one individual or party. The Senate filibuster guarantees recognition of minority viewpoints. One-party rule is dangerous unless there are safeguards to give the minority a voice. Citizens must constantly monitor and limit government power.

3) A FREE AND DIVERSIFIED MEDIA

Freedom of the press and freedom of speech are essential. If a group of politically like-minded news corporations control most of the media outlets, there is likely a monopoly that can be used to influence opinions. Our laws restrict news outlets from libel suits because they have investigative ability and are expected to present both sides of issues. When the news is no longer bipartisan, those laws should not apply. The tendency is to eliminate other opinions. With digital media, the challenge is even greater, as large single corporations (e. g. Google, Facebook, Twitter, etc.) can overwhelm competitors and control the flow of information to the public. Offensive speech is limited, and censorship begins. This is dangerous because opinions vary as to what is offensive and to whom. Even though Big Tech is run by private corporations, they can monopolize platforms and should be broken up to create competition.

Freedom of religion, decentralization of power, and a free and diversified media are all necessary to protect against government despotism. Societies which yield information control to others, government or corporations, may never get it back. Free speech is essential to keeping all our other freedoms.

STORIES & REFLECTIONS

WORRY

We usually worry about bad events that might happen to us in the future. Yet most of the time those bad outcomes never happen. If we can take action, we usually do, but events that we have no control over are the ones that can cause great stress. Stress can immobilize us and damage our immune response, things that do not help us. There are a few things that can be done to reduce worry:

LEARN ALL YOU CAN ABOUT THE SITUATION

Knowledge usually helps us to understand better the options we have, and to possibly take action. Study about your situation and look up solutions. Taking action reduces worry.

KEEP BUSY AND OCCUPIED IN OTHER ASPECTS OF YOUR LIFE

Unless it is life-threatening, there is more to life than what you worry about. Give your problem its' due attention, but don't just sit around and worry about it. Get on with life. Even with life-threatening conditions, imminent death is rare. Try to live one day at a time.

COMPARE YOURSELF TO OTHERS

This is about the only situation where this should be done. If we look around, we can always find people with worse or more serious problems than what we have. Count your blessings and try to help others less fortunate than you.

FOLLOW THE SERENITY PRAYER

"God, grant me the serenity to accept the things I cannot change, the courage to change the things I can, and the wisdom to know the difference". Your faith in God can be critical. This is one mantra worth memorizing!

STORIES & REFLECTIONS

WRESTLING AROUND

Back in the 1950s' and 1960s' it was common for guys to settle their disputes by wrestling, rather than fistfights, which were more violent. I was not a big aggressive type person, but in high school was once provoked into wrestling on the lawn at the entrance to Central High. I can't even remember the reason I did that, but I quickly ended up in the principals' office and my parents were notified. I don't remember my dad saying too much, and no injury occurred, but I think I held my own in the scuffle. I was only around 145 pounds, but very quick, which helped. I think we had a little exposure to team wrestling in high school gym, but I never took up the sport at that time.

When I got to the U of M and joined the Phi Sigma Kappa undergraduate fraternity, the brothers encouraged me to be on our Intra Mural wrestling team. By then I was still around 145 pounds and was told I would have no problem getting down below 139 pounds into the lighter weight class, which was an advantage. Food and water deprivation, strenuous workouts, sweating, etc. were all done, especially just before the weigh-in, but I didn't make the lower weight.

I was completely exhausted from trying to lose weight, and promptly lost my first match, which eliminated me from further competition!

My wrestling Coup d'état occurred when I was in Dental School and a member of the Delta Sigma Delta dental fraternity. I must have felt confident because I accepted a friendly wrestling challenge from a brother that was almost 1 ½ times my weight. Things went along smoothly until we all heard a "crack". I had broken a bone in my fraternity brothers' lower leg! Needless to say, I felt very bad about doing that, and didn't get more challenges or into any wrestling matches after that

Intra Mural sports was a popular activity at the U of Michigan in the 1960s'. Besides wrestling, I was on a fraternity tennis team and touch football team. I played a lineman in football and, although skinny and lightweight, could slither in between the big guys and tag out the runner!

STORIES & REFLECTIONS

GREAT-GRANDFATHER, DR. R E KLINESTEKER

My father was a quiet, strong-willed, and compassionate man that I looked up to very much. Many weekend mornings for years he would take me in the car somewhere or do something together like shopping at Fruit Basket on 28th street, go to the family farm, or visit Aunt Jenny and Henry Verhulst in Holland. A good description of him was written in the Michigan State Dental Society Journal of July, 1948.

One trait that demonstrated his true compassion was his ability to give a dental injection with little, if any discomfort. He was one of the first dentists in Grand Rapids to use "novacain" for dental fillings, even though it was routinely used for tooth extractions at the time. The article does not mention it, but he had a significant role in getting fluoride added to the city water to prevent tooth decay. Grand Rapids was the first city in the world to have that done, and the Grand Rapids study was a tremedous milestone in preventing dental decay. He was born in 1898. His first office in Grand Rapids at Burton Heights burned down, and then he moved to 216 Metz Building on Fulton.

My father enjoyed flower gardening, photography, politics, listening to classical music, and reading as hobbies. He was a fairly quiet, low-key person, but could have fun with the best, as he was a batchelor into his 30's. He would tell me stories of pranks he would play in college as well as many stories of on the farm growing up and his dog Shep. He had a good sense of humor. Literature, the classics, art, history, and motivation were some subjects he liked to read about.

Dr. R.E. Klinesteker

STORIES & REFLECTIONS

WATER FLUORIDATION STORY

Your great-grandfather, Dr. Russell Edward Klinesteker, played a significant role in getting Grand Rapids to be the first city in the world to add fluoride to its' water supply for the prevention of tooth decay.

THE PROBLEM: SEVERE

In the 1930's, dental decay was a serious, widespread, and life-threatening problem. It affected eating, digestion, speech, and could result in severe pain, even to the point of suicide. In those days, 98% of the population was affected by tooth decay, and 80% of children at 6 years of age had an average of 14 cavities. Dr Bill VerMeullen reported that he did hundreds of extractions and full dentures for teenagers with rotting stumps for teeth and was booked solid every Saturday morning! Many dentists of that time stated that around 75% of their practice consisted of just extractions and dentures. In 1938, only 6 apposing teeth were required to get into the military and 10% of draftees were rejected for dental reasons, the largest cause.

When that requirement was lifted during WW2, 40% of young draftees needed immediate treatment for dental pain! By age 55, half of all Americans needed full dentures.

THE STUDY: EXTENSIVE

In the early 1900's, people noticed stained teeth in otherwise healthy children of some Colorado towns, and research was done to find the cause of this "Colorado Brown Stain". It was found that high natural concentrations of fluoride ion in the water supply, up to 14 ppm, caused the stain and mottling of teeth during development. It was also noticed that their teeth were cavity-free, very rare in those days. Further research revealed that only 1 ppm of fluoride in the water supply gave cavity protection with no stain. Consequently, the US Public Health Service began working with the U of M research facilities to do a study. Grand Rapids was selected along with Muskegon as the control because they both had fluoride-free water. Your great grandfather was president of the West Michigan District Dental society in 1944 and made a convincing argument for the Grand Rapids City Council and Board of Education to accept the study, which started on January 25, 1945 and lasted for 15 years. Along with 150,000 dental exams, saliva samples urine samples, and X-Rays were taken.

THE RESULTS: AMAZING!

After 5 years, the fluoridated water in Grand Rapids had reduced dental decay by 60-65%! The results were so dramatic that Muskegon, the control city, dropped out of the study and fluoridated its' own water. The CDC has identified water fluoridation as one of the 10 greatest public health achievements of the 20th century. It is also one of the safest and least costly at $.31 cents per person annually. A lethal dose of fluoride is 5-10 grams. That is equivalent to drinking 10,000 8-ounce glasses of fluoridated water, all at once! "Steel Water" is a 33-foot tall metal sculpture by Cyril Lixenberg that was dedicated in 2007 honoring water fluoridation. It resides downtown on the Grand River in front of the Marriott Hotel.

There always have been some people opposed to mass medication. Today, there are still people that wish to not have government force them to ingest medical treatments or cures, and in a free society, that is fair to responsible adults. With fluoridation, people can choose fluoride-free toothcare products and drink bottled or well water. Yet, largely because of the use of fluoride-free bottled water, tooth decay incidence has increased. In a free society, the best role of government should be to educate and make available disease preventing treatments, not mandate their enforcement. With this article, I hope to emphasize the importance of fluoridated water and let people choose what is best for them.

Grand Rapids Fluoridation Sculpture

STORIES & REFLECTIONS

IMMUNE SYSTEM IMPORTANCE

Your immune system is key to a long healthy life. It is wise to develop healthy habits early in life that protect you against infections. Because our bodies' main defense against viral and bacterial infections is our immune system, it only makes sense to do things to enhance it, or at least to avoid behaviors that harm it, especially during times of a virus pandemic. I recently saw on WEBMD.com a list of common behaviors that people do to suppress their immune system and leave them more susceptible to infection. There is much anxiety and blaming out there concerning the Covid-19 pandemic, but the most important thing to remember is that there are things we can do or avoid to enhance our own resistance to it.

THINGS THAT SUPRESS YOUR IMMUNE SYSTEM

1) LACK OF SLEEP – Sleep is critical in allowing our immune system to renew itself. Take a nap, break, or postpone something. Don't sweat the small stuff.
2) ANXIETY – Will affect your susceptibility to infection. Being lonely, fearful, or stressed can cause anxiety. It is helpful to study and learn as much as possible about what you fear to reduce anxiety.
3) LOW VITAMIN D – Can cause many problems and will affect the immune system. Eating eggs, salmon, fortified milk, and getting some sunshine can help.
4) SOME MEDICATIONS – Corticosteroids, chemotherapy, and anti-inflammatory drugs are some that could affect immunity. Use them sparingly or check with your doctor about alternatives.
5) NOT ENOUGH FRESH FRUITS AND VEGETABLES – A balanced, healthy diet is known to support a strong immune system. Fruits and vegetables contain many complex compounds that boost our immunity.
6) MARIJUANA – Can alter the immune function and decrease host resistance to viruses as well as bacterial agents. Smoking it can especially cause lung inflammation and breathing problems.
7) HIGH FAT DIET – Bacon, pork, and red meats can increase the incidence of obesity. Obese and diabetic people often have a higher incidence of flu and other infections.
8) LITTLE TIME OUTDOORS – Sunshine and fresh outside air help bolster our immune systems.

9) SMOKING, TOBACCO USE, AND VAPING – All are known to suppress our immune system responses.
10) ALCOHOL – Excess alcohol consumption has long been known to result in slower and less complete recovery from infection, higher postoperative complications, and poor wound healing.
11) GRIEF AND SORROW – Long lasting grief can cause a stress hormone imbalance that leaves people prone to infections. Professional help is recommended.
12) LACK OF EXERCISE – This may be the most important factor of all. Good total body circulation is needed to effect wide distribution of antibodies and white blood cells that fight infections.
13) FEW CLOSE, LOVING RELATIONSHIPS – Positive emotional relationships with friends, family and spouse can heal in more ways than one. Work towards reconciliation.
14) LOW HUMIDITY LEVELS – I felt this important to add. Studies show that low humidity levels in the air increases viral transmission. 40% - 60% is ideal. Heated winter indoor air is unusually well below that, and humidification is recommended.

Rather than blaming others regarding pandemics, we all need to take personal responsibility and offer solutions, beginning with ourselves. Blaming others does not solve anything and divides us, making things worse. It is best to be a positive example for your friends.

STORIES & REFLECTIONS

LANGUAGE AND WRITING SKILLS

Not everyone enjoys writing. In high school English class my grades were acceptable at best. I did not enjoy reading fiction stories, although I did enjoy reading about science. It was rare for me to write even a short note, let alone a long letter to a friend or my parents when away. When I spent 2 months in Germany as an exchange student, I began to realize how important writing and language are, and I really looked forward to receiving letters from home. I then started writing some letters back home and keeping a diary. Putting thoughts down on paper is really the most effective and accurate way to communicate due to its permanence. What is said or written on the Internet or social media has far less credence than a hand-written letter or published book on facts.

BETTER COMMUNICATION

Expressing your feelings and describing situations accurately is very important. Even voice inflection can convey meaning to the spoken word. The English language is what we use in America to communicate with each other, and it is wise to develop language skills to more effectively connect with people. English can be a difficult language to learn for people that speak other languages, but you have a head start because you spoke it as a child. Your effectiveness and success in adult life depends greatly on your ability to communicate with others. Spelling, grammar, and even articulation skills all help you convey your thoughts, ideas, and intentions to others. To use vulgar, negative or improper language is easier, but can be a turn-off for many people. It could be called "lazy language" when slang, vulgar words or poor grammar are used excessively. Most people are not impressed with that at all. Language is a reflection of culture, and there are many dialects in most languages. All should be respected and given equal treatment. It is not racist to speak or write properly in any language, just better communication.

DIGITAL HINDERENCE/HELP

Texting is one thing that can help destroy a persons' language skills, where grammar, punctuation, and spelling all take a back seat to brevity. That should be countered with enough accurate writing experience to maintain good communication skills. Writing letters, keeping a diary, or writing articles about your interests all can help with that. I highly recommend the use of todays' computer word processors. They can help by correcting your errors in spelling, grammar, and punctuation so that you are learning as you write. Also, Word processors allow the writer to easily proof-read and change the wording for better understanding.

YOUR FUTURE

Applying for a job interview is a prime example of the importance of language skills to your future success. Imagine if your job application resume' had just a couple of words misspelled and how that might impact your chances of being hired! If it pays to put special attention to something like that, why don't all our other communications receive the same scrutiny? It just makes sense. Using proper English, speaking or writing, needs to become a habit. Innate language skills are developed from friends, family, and school classes. So, even though English classes may seem boring and unproductive now, you can be rest assured that you are learning skills that will serve you well over a lifetime!

Made in USA - Kendallville, IN
67443_9798402836181
04.26.2022 1601